CAMPSIE WARE

The story of a distinctive type of ornamental
Scottish pottery of the later 20th century

GRAEME CRUICKSHANK
MA, AMA, FMA, FSA Scot

SCOTTISH POTTERY STUDIES No. 3

GLASGOW CITY
LIBRARIES

1992

Previous titles in the series:-

No.1 Scottish Spongeware (out of print)

No. 2 Scottish Saltglaze

SCOTTISH POTTERY STUDIES

No.3 Campsie Ware

ISBN 0-906169-36-4

Cover illustration:
Scottie dog mantle-piece ornament. Height 5 inches.

Foreword

SCOTTISH POTTERY STUDIES is the name given to a series of booklets, the aim of each being to examine some specific aspect of Scottish Pottery history. The scheme was initiated in 1980 as a result of a bequest from Frank E. Cruickshank of Aberdeen, and the first booklets in what was intended to be a regular series appeared in 1982. This author researched, compiled, scripted, designed, produced, and distributed the booklets, but the high cost of printing and the involved mechanics of marketing has meant that the series has not progressed with the regularity originally anticipated. I am, therefore, very grateful to Glasgow City Libraries for taking over the production and distribution of this latest booklet, which has allowed the series to progress. This is quite appropriate, for Glasgow was unquestionably the principal centre of production of the once-thriving Scottish pottery industry. The black and white photographs were kindly supplied by Mrs Langley, and although the quality is not very good, they were included as they are the only photographs in existence of Campsie Ware in production, and for that we are grateful. I would also like to thank the staff of The Mitchell Library, particularly Karen Cunningham of the Publications Board; Moira Thorburn, Photographer; and Verina Litster, Graphic Designer, for their efforts in bringing the notion of a booklet on Campsie Ware to reality.

G.D.R.C.
Edinburgh, June 1992

FROM TELEPHONE : 041 882 1711

CAMPSIE WARE

POTTERY MANUFACTURERS

29-31 LISTER ROAD, HILLINGTON
GLASGOW, S.W.2

MESSRS.

PER

CAMPSIE WARE

Introduction

In the early 1980s, a type of pottery ware started to appear among the older, more established names of Scottish pottery production, firstly on bric-a-brac stalls and in second-hand shops, then at collectors' fairs and in antique shops. Mantle-piece ornaments for the most part, the striking yet subtle colouring of these items made them eye-catching and collectable. They generally bore the mark "Campsie Ware Scotland", yet no pottery has ever existed in the vicinity of the Campsie Fells which could account for such a volume of production. I was mystified, and so apparently were many other Scottish pottery enthusiasts, judging by the letters of enquiry which came in to Scottish Pottery Studies.

The breakthrough came a couple of years ago, thanks to my good friends Murdo and Jo McEwan. Jo's parents reside at Milton of Campsie, and on one of their visits there, Murdo got the scent of this unheralded brand of Scottish pottery. This set me on the trail, leading to the former home, and last work-place, of the proprietor of Campsie Ware, Mr Edward Langley, situated on the outskirts of Milton of Campsie. He had died in 1982, but his widow, Mrs Marigold Langley, still lived there. I am very grateful to her, and to one of their sons, Mr George Langley, himself a potter, for supplying much of the information upon which this book is based.

Portrait photograph of Edward Langley.

The origins of Campsie Ware

It is now widely recognised that the products of the old Scottish potteries constitute a distinctive element in the field of Scottish material culture. One type of ware of more recent origin which is currently attracting attention - not because it is distinctively Scottish, but because it is both Scottish and distinctive - is Campsie Ware. It was produced by Edward Langley, who originally came from Liverpool. Although he had no formal artistic training, he had a strong leaning towards sculpture, which he produced in various media - wood, slate, stone, and even coal brickettes!

Humble beginnings - Ted Langley's first kiln, at Glorat in the Campsie Fells, which he built himself. It operated between 1946 and 1949.

After the Second World War, he and his wife Marigold moved to her family home of Glorat, near the Campsie Fells in Stirlingshire. Edward Langley was at this time working for the Ministry of Food, but he yielded to his artistic temperament, and began to make pottery on a part-time basis. It was hardly an auspicious start, for he built his first kiln on a rubbish tip, and fired it using household waste, and also coal waste - in the days of cheap coal, big houses with many fire-places and/or coal-fired central heating used much fuel, and he found that by digging deep, he could recover large pieces of good coal which had been thrown out with the ashes. Here he produced small slip-cast ornaments, sometimes using local clay, and sold them door-to-door from a suitcase.

These early pieces (which were not marked, and are therefore hard to identify nowadays) were well received by his customers, and his cute little animals - Scottie dogs, bunnies, toads, fish, etc - found a ready market. This success encouraged him to give up his government job and become a full-time potter. The obvious place to go to secure employment was Glasgow, but the great days of the Glasgow pottery industry were over by this time. From being a significant part of the city's economy in Victorian times, it had waned almost to the point of extinction. One firm continued to prosper, however, and that was the Govancroft Pottery. One of the newer Glasgow potteries - it was founded about 1911 - it succeeded in surviving the Depression and the war years, and thrived thereafter by switching the emphasis of its stoneware production from heavy commercial goods to table ware.

Edward Langley joined the staff of Govancroft Pottery in 1949. His inventive sense of design created a series of small novelty goods, such as a pottery book, complete with leather-covered pseudo-spine entitled *The Spirit of Scotland*; a small cork revealed its true contents - the spirit of Scotland all right, but in the form not of words but of liquor - Paterson's De Luxe Scotch Whisky! His aptitude for creating such popular novelties led to rapid promotion, and within a couple of years he had risen to become works manager.

However, Edward Langley quickly became frustrated with an establishment to which he contributed a great deal in the way of new ideas but from which he did not receive what he considered to be his due credit, and so in 1952 he decided to take the bold step of establishing his own pottery. This was none too easy to achieve, however, for it transpired that several members of the licensing board to whom he applied were also directors of Govancroft Pottery, and they looked none too kindly upon the prospect of a rival concern being established in the city. In the end, he got his licence - and also a month's notice from his employers, so there was no chance for any last-minute change of plan. He was now committed to setting himself up as an independent potter.

Campsie Ware production

Central Glasgow is where Edward Langley (known as Ted to family and friends) established his pottery in the autumn of 1952, in premises formerly occupied by the St. Vincent Glass Company at 130 Pitt Street. He used a gas-fired kiln, and continued his speciality of making slip-cast ornaments. Three years later, however, he was compelled to close down the works when that area of the city was redeveloped, and so in 1955 he moved to 29/31 Lister Road in Hillington, an industrial area in the south-west of Glasgow, where he set up in premises formerly occupied by Western Preserves Ltd.

Here the firm was to thrive for the next twenty years. It operated with two electric kilns, and Mr Langley employed five or six people at the pottery. Small novelty goods, manufactured by the slip-cast process, continued to be the mainstay of production, posy vases and miniature whisky barrels being a speciality. Another item, a miniature cauldron, is reminiscent of Dunmore and Wemyss wares of last century.

Much of the Hillington production bears a strong resemblance to that of Govancroft Pottery, and this was no mere coincidence. Two reasons account for the similarity. Firstly, Ted Langley felt that he was morally entitled to use the designs which he had devised while employed at Govancroft, and several lines are common to both potteries, having very little difference between them. Secondly, a number of Govancroft potters came to work for Ted Langley, including the chief mould-maker and several experienced women casters, following a disastrous fire which caused Govancroft Pottery to cease production for some considerable time.

Thistle-shaped posy vases; the smallest was reputedly used as a dram measure. Height of biggest 3.2 inches.

Thistle-shaped cruet sets; the smaller pair have a thistle-shaped tray. Height of biggest 3.9 inches.

Budgerigar mantle-piece ornaments, both single and paired. Height of bigger 6 inches.

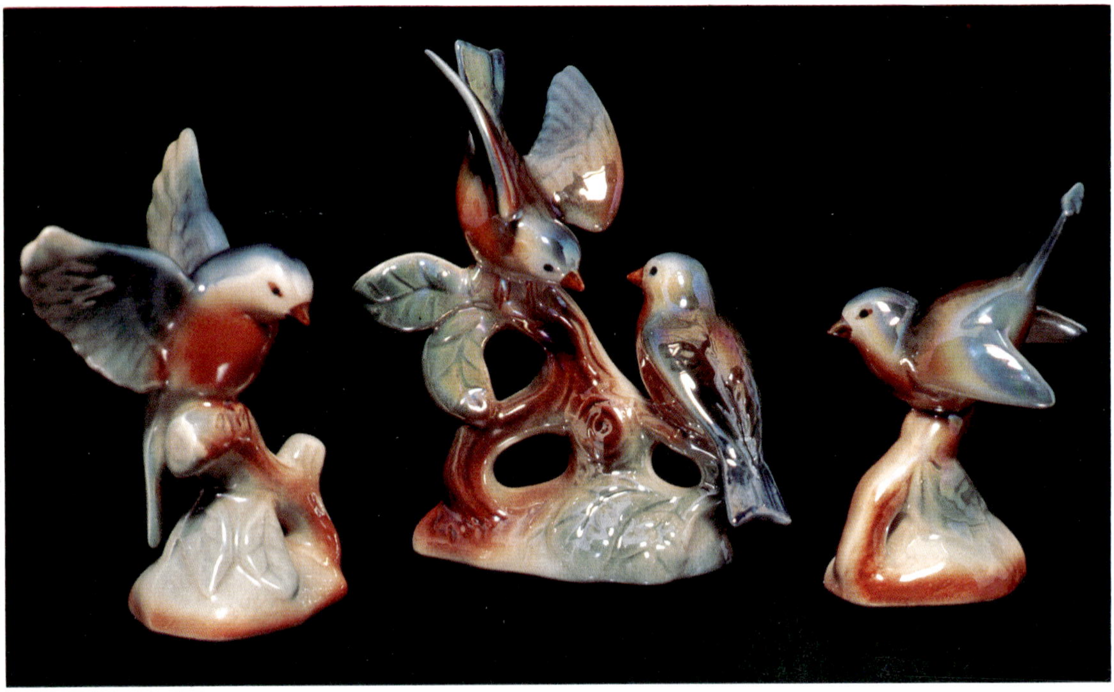

Chaffinch mantle-piece ornaments, both single and paired, plus an unusual example of a bird with outstretched wings. Height of biggest 6.8 inches.

Macaw and stork mantle-piece ornaments.
Height of bigger 10.8 inches.

Trout and perch mantle-piece ornaments.
Height of bigger 5.4 inches.

Log-shaped posy vases featuring long-eared rabbits.
Height of biggest 3.8 inches.

Tourist souvenirs: two tree-stump-shaped posy vases, one featuring a rabbit from Turriff, the other a squirrel from Buckie; a barrel-shaped posy vase from Aberdeen; a bluebird mantle-piece ornament from Rothesay; and a milk jug from Leven.
Height of biggest 4.5 inches.

This influx of workers was both welcome and necessary, for the growing popularity of his products meant that Langley had not the time to perform or be constantly involved in all the operations of the pottery himself. Seeking an identity for his works, and mindful of the location where his first tentative efforts had borne fruit, he chose the name 'Campsie'. He could hardly call his factory the Campsie Pottery, situated as it was in the city of Glasgow, but he termed its products 'Campsie Ware', and this became the firm's trade name.

The Campsie Ware factory at Hillington in Glasgow. Note the lack of a name-board or any form of advertising - for some reason, Ted Langley was superstitious about such things!

From this time, and continuing throughout the 1960s, one of the principal lines of production was naturalistic three-dimensional thistle-shaped goods. These consisted of various domestic containers, and in their style, form, and colour, these items of Campsie Ware are virtually indistinguishable from the Highland Ware of the Govancroft Pottery. To complicate matters further, some items of the Cowal Ware of the West Highland Pottery in Dunoon are near-identical to both!

Cruets, small jars, dram measures, and the like were made to resemble thistles. The larger Campsie salt and pepper shakers were free-standing, while the smaller ones sat in pottery trays, themselves mimicking the thistle shape. (An alternative cruet design, presumably made for English consumption, consisted of salt and pepper shakers resembling acorns, sitting on an oak-leaf tray.) There were even peat-reekers, made for an enterprising Helensburgh entrepreneur named Gordon McBeth, which were much favoured by Americans who wished to savour the tang of Highland air when back in their homeland. The thistle ware goods were marketed in tartan boxes - just as was done at Govancroft.

A further example of utilising a Govancroft style, not so much in the shape but in the method of decoration, was the application of colour by means of a loose and fluffy sponge to give an all-over speckled effect. This method was mainly used on jugs and vases.

Another line was introduced around this time which was the most distinctive of all, and which was to bring Campsie Ware its principal accolades, being eagerly bought in its own day and avidly collected now. This was a series of figurines, mainly of birds, spray-painted in a bright but subtle range of colours, and given a special glaze which imparted to them an iridescent splendour. The birds were designed by a sculptor, Henry Paulin, who was a Royal Academician, while Ted Langley designed the stands on which they perched, usually branches or stumps.

The stands not only had to be artistically pleasing but also fashioned to allow ease of handling during the colour spraying process. Here Ted Langley was operating under a considerable handicap, for, as the result of a nasty accident at the age of three involving an item of agricultural machinery, he had completely lost three fingers of his right hand - and he was right-handed. However, he became very dextrous with his remaining index finger and thumb.

The bird figurines were decorated by means of a pressurised air device known as an aerograph, at least four colours, which were merged subtly together, being used on each item. The spraying was done directly onto the raw unfired clay, with features such as the bills, claws, and eyes being painted in by brush. The figurines were then dipped in a transparent glaze, and fired. After that, they were sprayed with a lustre and fired again at a very low temperature, resulting in a glittering iridescence of striking appearance. This is without any direct parallel in the whole field of ceramic production in Britain to my knowledge. The iridescent glaze is rather similar to some of the Art Deco products of Glasgow's Britannia Pottery in the 1920s, and to part of the output of some Stoke-on-Trent works, such as the Byzanta Ware of Grimwade's and the Crown Devon Ware of Fielding & Co. However, the only direct comparison with the spray-glazing of bird figurines and suchlike ornaments which I have seen is supplied by Jema Ware, a product of Holland.

These Campsie bird figurines became very popular, especially the smaller ones such as chaffinches, robins, budgerigars, kingfishers, and bluebirds, both singles and pairs. At the peak of production, moulds were re-used so many times that details such as feathers tended to become somewhat ill-defined. It apparently became a standing joke with the pottery workers that the boss would keep on making birds until they looked like frogs! Ted Langley's sculptural leanings manifested themselves in an alternative style which he occasionally employed, where figures such as a duck in flight, and an elegantly-draped female, were depicted in a somewhat stylised form. These he tended to decorate with only a single uniform colour, or even leave plain white. They were not normally production pieces, but made in very limited numbers for members of his family.

Campsie figurines (mostly birds, occasionally fish) were the most popular of the firm's products, but another line which achieved almost the same status was a type of miniature posy vase modelled to represent a log or stump, beside or on which crouches a woodland animal such as a rabbit or squirrel. Usually the piece of tree and the animal are rendered in contrasting colours. There are direct parallels here with some English products, notably the Sylvac Ware of Shaw & Copestake of Longton in Staffordshire, and the Fauna Ware made by the Hornsea Pottery and the Eastgate Pottery at Withernsea, both in Yorkshire.

Because of the popularity of these various products they were marked with the firm's name by means of a rubber stamp. This reads 'CAMPSIE WARE' or 'CAMPSIE WARE SCOTLAND'; and such marks always appear in black. Sometimes the base bottoms were glazed, leaving only the footrim unglazed, and this indicates an early piece; later the whole of the underside was left unglazed.

A flock of pigeons lines up, awaiting the aerograph to enliven the colour of their plumage. More bird ornaments are assembled on the drying racks in the background. Above the chair in the centre, a mixing tub for slip may be seen, while above the chair on the left is a large thistle-shaped jug which appears to have been used for pouring slip. Moulds filled with slip (the bindings are clearly visible) are stacked up to the left of the jug, and may also be seen at the back on the right.

A mustering of stately storks, patiently awaiting their turn at being glazed. Two female operatives keep production flowing.

Around this time, another line was produced which has been the subject of some confusion - at least in the mind of this writer, until the explanation made matters clear. There is a range of ware which appears to be very similar to Govancroft/Campsie products, yet from its markings it would seem to be of English manufacture. It consists mainly of small ornaments, and is known as Dee-Cee ware. The explanation is that it was commissioned from Campsie by an English agent named D.C. Cooper, who wanted his own trade-name to appear on the goods which he marketed. Langley was happy to oblige, and so these pieces bear the rubber-stamped mark "Dee-Cee England", but they really are a division of Campsie Ware.

The growing popularity of Campsie Ware and the ever-increasing range of its retail outlets led it to becoming an accepted form of tourist souvenir. Figures, posy vases, and tea items were sometimes embellished with the names of resort towns, not just in Scotland but in England and Ireland as well. Thus Campsie products found a new market and an ever wider area of circulation.

A full kiln of newly-fired Campsie Ware. Two types of bird ornament predominate, with a fair sprinkling of thistle-shaped salt and pepper shakers.

Campsie Ware returns home

In 1975, Langley's twenty-year lease of the Hillington factory came to an end. In all that time, there had been no rent increase, but now Ted Langley was faced with a massive rise. He therefore decided to move, and returned to his old stamping ground, setting up at West Baldoran Farm on the outskirts of Milton of Campsie, not far from the scene of his first efforts at pottery-making in the late 1940s. However, this was a considerably scaled-down version of his previous enterprise. He brought one of the electric kilns from Hillington with him, and established himself at Campsie in a one-man operation in a semi-retired capacity.

While at Baldoran, Ted Langley saw one of his sons also enter the pottery business. The second of his three sons, George, established the Cromlech Pottery Co. Ltd. in Cumbernauld in 1977, running it until 1985. He brought to it the same dedication and industry that his father had shown. However, he lacked support of the same calibre, and he was quite exhausted when he eventually sold up, though he left with a full order book and a reputation for meticulous care regarding the quality of his products. George Langley specialised in making ceramic lamp-bases, and his large turnover meant that he could be of some assistance to his father, helping with supplies of clay and with the storage and delivery of the manufactured goods. Having been raised in the pottery business, George was well steeped in its working practices, and required no formal training.

Although the operation at West Baldoran Farm was small-scale compared with the Hillington venture, Ted Langley nonetheless established a going production pottery. He adapted the new byre by taking out the stall dividers along one wall, and filling in one of the grepes using old kiln bats. Here he installed the better of the kilns from his previous premises, and fitted up the other necessary equipment. In terms of production, he returned to some of the favoured lines of the past, such as thistle-shaped condiment containers. His aptitude for novelty in design was still a functioning force, and other containers assumed various guises, such as a miniature curling stone which turns out to be a whisky flask when the handle is removed, and a tam-o'-shanter bonnet which masks a butter dish. Most of these items are unmarked; occasionally some are rubber-stamped with the slogan "Made in Scotland". Plainer items such as lamp-bases were also made, decorated with single strong colours.

Ted Langley continued to be a practising potter right up until the time of his death in 1982. Indeed, he left behind a half-finished kiln-load, the firing of which was completed by his son George. This did not mark the end of pottery production at West Baldoran Farm, however, for in the following year, 1983, the pottery was taken over by David Norman, who produced large sculptural vases and the like, using crank (heavily-grogged clay), until early in 1989. Now part of the former pottery is occupied by a blacksmith's workshop.

Visiting West Baldoran Farm today, much of Ted Langley's pottery still remains to be seen. His kiln is gone, replaced by a new electric one by Norman, but most of his other equipment is still there in the new byre - the blunger, used to break down the raw clay (in this case, made from an oil drum!); the agitator, used to prepare the slip; and the aerograph booth, made by De Vilbis of London, where the spray decoration was done. Sitting around are various sieves, bags of glaze colours (supplied by G.J. Bains of Stoke), and many of the standard six-foot boards used for carrying the partly-completed ware from one process to another - some of these were acquired from the Victoria Pottery in Pollokshaws when it closed down in 1952.

In the old byre, which was used as a store, are dozens of moulds. Some of these are block moulds *i.e.* first-generation moulds, from which the production moulds were fabricated. Among them are many of the well-loved bird figurines, and also some which were little used because of their complexity, such as the donkey and cart. In these stacks of white plaster moulds, slowly accruing a covering of dust, the story of Campsie Ware may still be read.

Ted Langley succeeded as a production potter, in an era when most Scottish ceramic goods came from the kilns of craft potters, because of his technical skill and his marketing acumen. With a wife and family depending on his ability to run a profitable business, he took the trouble to seek out what people wanted, and then targeted a market where he knew that a desire for his products already existed. The other element in his strategy was to maintain a high standard of production, and the consistent technical quality of his wares regularly won him repeat orders.

As to the artistic merits of Campsie Ware, this calls for a subjective appraisal which is more difficult to make in view of constantly-changing public taste. Popular in the 50s and 60s, regarded as outmoded, even 'naff', in the 70s and 80s, it is now achieving a new level of appreciation. One pointer to this development is that items of Campsie Ware are beginning to percolate through from the bric-a-brac stalls to the antique shops. Perhaps it does all date from the second half of the 20th century, but it has become one of the most collectable types of Scottish pottery in the 1990s, and soon Campsie Ware will be able to stand among the ranks of those products which are recognised and appreciated as part of Scotland's ceramic heritage.